The Best
SALADS &
LIGHT MEALS

The Best
SALADS &
LIGHT MEALS

Pastas, Sandwiches, Salads,
Entrées, and Other Delightful Bites

By Gregg R. Gillespie

BLACK DOG
& LEVENTHAL
PUBLISHERS
NEW YORK

Published by
Black Dog & Leventhal Publishers, Inc.
151 West 19th Street
New York, NY 10011

Distributed by
Workman Publishing
708 Broadway
New York, NY 10003

Manufactured in Spain

ISBN 1-57912-294-9

Library of Congress Cataloging-in-Publication Data is on file and available
from Black Dog & Leventhal Publishers, Inc.

Cover and interior design by 27.12 Design, Ltd.
Interior layout by Cindy Joy
Photography by Peter Barry

g f e d c b a

CONTENTS

APPLE AND FENNEL
SALAD

makes 6 servings

5 oz. fresh spinach,
washed, trimmed and torn
into bite-sized pieces
1 small head of fennel, sliced
2 medium Granny Smith
apples, peeled, cored and
diced

1 small red onion, sliced
½ cup dressing of choice

In a bowl, combine the spinach, fennel, apples and onion. Drizzle on the
dressing and serve.

BEET AND POTATO SALAD

makes 4 to 6 servings

¼ cup oil and vinegar dressing
4 tsp. ground coriander
3 medium-sized red-skinned
  potatoes, cooked and sliced

3 beets, cooked and sliced
Salt and pepper to taste

1. In a small bowl, blend together the dressing and coriander.
2. In another bowl, blend together the potatoes and beets. Blend in the dressing, season to taste and serve.

CAULIFLOWER
SALAD

makes 6 to 8 servings

1 medium head of cauliflower, trimmed and cored
2 cups prepared guacamole

½ cup shredded Cheddar cheese
Radish roses

1. In a saucepan, cover the cauliflower with 1 cup of lightly salted water. Bring to a boil and cook for about 15 to 20 minutes or until tender.
2. Place the cauliflower in a bowl, cover with plastic wrap and refrigerate for about 1 hour. Top with the guacamole, sprinkle on the cheese, garnish with radish roses, and serve.

CHICKEN AND APPLE
SALAD
makes 4 to 6 servings

4 cups cooked chicken, diced   1 cup celery, diced
2 cups Macintosh apples, diced   ½ cup mayonnaise

In a bowl, combine the chicken, apples, celery and mayonnaise.
Cover with plastic wrap and refrigerate for at least 2 hours before serving.

CHICKEN AND PINEAPPLE SALAD

makes about 1 serving

½ cup canned crushed
pineapple, drained

10 oz. cooked chicken, flaked
4 tbsp. mayonnaise

In a bowl, combine the pineapple, chicken and mayonnaise. Cover with plastic wrap and refrigerate for at least 2 hours before serving.

CHICKEN SALAD
WITH GRAPES

makes about 4 servings

4 cups salad greens, torn into
    bite-size pieces and chilled
10 oz. cooked chicken, flaked

1 cup seedless grapes, halved
½ cup bottled Italian dressing

In a bowl, toss the salad greens, chicken, grapes, and dressing. Cover with
plastic wrap and refrigerate for about 1 hour before serving.

CILANTRO SLAW
WITH GARLIC DRESSING

makes about 6 servings

1 small head of cabbage,
   finely shredded
2 tbsp. fresh cilantro, minced
1 medium cucumber,
   peeled, seeded and
   cut into 3-inch pieces

1 small yellow onion, minced
½ cup bottled garlic
   salad dressing

In a bowl, toss the cabbage, cilantro, cucumbers, onion, and salad dressing.
Cover with plastic wrap and refrigerate for about 1 hour before serving.

FRESH VEGETABLE SALAD

makes 6 to 8 servings

1 tbsp. tarragon leaves, snipped
2 cups broccoli florettes

2 cups cauliflower florettes
½ cup Italian-style dressing
Salt and pepper to taste

In a bowl, blend together the tarragon, broccoli, and cauliflower. Drizzle on the dressing and cover with plastic wrap. Refrigerate for at least 1 hour. Adjust the seasoning to taste and serve.

GERMAN-STYLE CABBAGE SALAD

makes 6 to 8 servings

½ pound bacon
2 cups red onions, chopped
½ cup cider vinegar

1 medium head of cabbage,
cored and shredded

In a skillet, sauté the bacon until crisp. Transfer to a rack covered with paper towels and crumble. In the same skillet, sauté the onions until tender and lightly colored. Add the vinegar, turn heat to low, and add the cabbage and bacon, tossing lightly to incorporate. Remove from the heat and serve.

GERMAN CHICKEN SALAD

makes 6 to 8 servings

1½ cups cooked chicken, shredded

1 can (8 oz.) crushed pineapple, drained

1 can (13 oz.) green peas, drained

1 cup mayonnaise

Salt and pepper to taste

In a bowl, combine the chicken, pineapple, peas, and mayonnaise. Season to taste and serve.

GRAPE AND GRAPEFRUIT SALAD

makes 4 servings

2 large ripe grapefruits
2 cups black grapes

¼ cup bottled French dressing
1 tbsp. fresh parsley, snipped

1. Cut the grapefruits in half and remove the segments. Reserve the rind.
2. In a bowl, combine the grapes and grapefruit. Drizzle on the dressing, cover with plastic wrap and refrigerate for at least 2 hours. Place the fruit mixture in the reserved grapefruit rinds, garnish with parsley, and serve.

HAWAIIAN
COUNTRY SLAW

makes 4 to 6 servings

1 can (20 oz.) pineapple
  chunks, drained
1 package (16 oz.) cole slaw
  salad mix

½ cup sunflower seeds
½ cup dressing of choice

In a bowl, combine the pineapple, coleslaw mix, and sunflower seeds.
Drizzle on the dressing, cover with plastic wrap and refrigerate
for at least 2 hours before serving.

JICAMA-SPINACH SALAD

makes 6 servings

8 cups loosely packed
spinach leaves, torn into
bite-size pieces
1 cup fresh strawberries, sliced

1 medium jicama, peeled,
cut into julienne strips
½ cup dressing of choice

In a bowl, combine the spinach, strawberries and jicama. Cover with plastic wrap and refrigerate for at least 1 hour. Drizzle on the dressing before serving.

ORANGE AND CHICORY
SALAD

makes 4 servings

1 bunch chicory (about 8 oz.),
  trimmed and thinly sliced
1 large Valencia orange,
  peeled and separated
  into segments

½ cup seedless grapes, halved
¼ cup bottled French dressing
Salt and pepper to taste

In a bowl, toss the chicory, orange segments, and grapes with the dressing, and season to taste. Cover with plastic wrap and refrigerate for about 1 hour before serving.

ORIENTAL PASTA SALAD

makes 4 servings

2 cups broccoli florettes
1½ cups cooked spaghetti
¾ cup red bell pepper,
   thinly sliced

2 tbsp. soy sauce
1 tbsp. sesame oil

1. In a bamboo steamer over a pot of boiling water, steam the broccoli for about 5 minutes or until just tender.
2. In a bowl, combine the broccoli, spaghetti, peppers, soy sauce, and oil. Cover with plastic wrap and refrigerate for at least 2 hours before serving.

PEA SALAD
FRANÇAISE
makes 4 servings

2 packages (10 oz. each)
  frozen green peas,
  thawed and drained
1 mint leaf
¼ cup olive oil

2 tbsp. red wine vinegar
1 medium garlic clove, minced
1 small head of lettuce, sliced
4 scallions, trimmed,
  (white part only)

1. In a saucepan, cover the peas with water and bring them to a boil.
   Add the mint leaf and cook for 15 to 20 minutes or until tender.
   Drain and rinse under cold water.
2. In a small bowl, blend together the oil and vinegar.
3. In another bowl, combine the garlic, lettuce, peas, and scallions.
   Drizzle on oil mixture, cover with plastic wrap and refrigerate for
   about 1 hour before serving.

PEPPER AND OLIVE SALAD

makes 4 servings

1 large red bell pepper, stemmed, halved and seeded

1 large green bell pepper, stemmed, halved and seeded

3 garlic cloves, chopped

¼ cup vegetable oil

18 pimiento-stuffed green olives, sliced

Parsley, chopped

1. Position the broiler rack about 6 inches from the heat.
2. Place the peppers on the broiler tray and broil for about 8 to 10 minutes or until the skin starts to sear. Place under running water, pull off the skins, and dice.
3. In a skillet, sauté the peppers and garlic in oil for about 2 minutes. Reduce to a very low simmer and cover. Cook, stirring occasionally, for about 15 minutes or until tender and thoroughly heated.
4. Pour the entire mixture, including the oil, into a bowl. Cool to room temperature and add the olives. Cover with plastic wrap and refrigerate for at least 1 hour. Garnish with parsley, and serve.

PICKLED BEETS
WITH CUCUMBERS

makes 2 servings

1 cup pickled beets
¼ cup red onion, thinly sliced

¾ cup seedless cucumber, diced
2 tsp. fresh dill weed, chopped

In a bowl, combine the beets, onion, cucumber, and dill weed.
Cover with plastic wrap and refrigerate until ready to serve.

PICKLED CUCUMBER
SALAD

makes 4 to 6 servings

1 large cucumber
Salt to taste
3 tbsp. vinegar

2 tbsp. sugar
Pepper, to taste
Dill weed, snipped

1. Trim the ends from the cucumber and score down the sides with a
   fork. Using a sharp knife cut into thin diagonal slices, sprinkle with
   salt, place in a plastic bag, seal, and refrigerate for about 2 hours.
2. Place the slices on a flat surface covered with paper towels and press
   all of the moisture from them. Transfer to a bowl.
3. Combine the vinegar and the sugar, and salt and pepper to taste.
   Drizzle over the cucumber slices, toss to coat, and garnish with dill weed.
   Serve immediately.

RADISH AND CELERY SALAD

makes 4 servings

1 cup radishes
1 cup celery, thinly sliced
¼ cup bottled French dressing

1 cup lettuce leaves,
   torn into bite-size pieces

In a bowl, combine the radishes, celery, and dressing. Cover with plastic wrap, and refrigerate for at least 1 hour. Top with the lettuce leaves and serve.

RAISIN CARROT SALAD

makes 4 to 6 servings

1 cup seedless raisins
1½ cup carrots, shredded
½ cup celery, minced
½ cup pecans or hazelnuts,
  chopped

¼ cup mayonnaise
Salt and pepper to taste

In a bowl, combine the raisins, carrots, celery, pecans and mayonnaise and season to taste. Cover with plastic wrap and refrigerate for about 1 hour before serving.

SPICY CABBAGE
SALAD

makes 4 servings

4 dried red peppers	1 teaspoon sesame oil
¼ teaspoon soy sauce	1 small head of cabbage,
¼ teaspoon rice wine vinegar	cut into bite-size pieces

1. In the container of a blender or food processor, combine the peppers, soy sauce, and vinegar. Add the sesame oil and process on high speed until smooth.
2. In a saucepan, cook the mixture for about 2 minutes. Blend in the cabbage and cook for about 10 minutes or until just tender.
3. Pour the mixture into a bowl, cover with plastic wrap and refrigerate for about 1 day before serving.

SPINACH AND BACON SALAD

makes 6 servings

2 garlic cloves, quartered
¾ cup bottled French dressing
2 bunches of spinach,
   torn into bite-size pieces

8 bacon slices,
   fried and crumbled

1. In a small bowl, blend together the garlic and the dressing.
   Cover with plastic wrap and refrigerate for about 2 hours.
2. In a bowl, toss the spinach and the bacon with the dressing and serve.

SPRING
SALAD

makes 4 servings

1 can (16 oz.) grapefruit
  sections, drained
4 scallions, trimmed
  and thinly sliced

½ cup radishes, sliced
½ cup cucumbers, sliced
½ cup bottled Roquefort
  or other creamy dressing

In a bowl, combine the grapefruit, scallions, radishes, cucumbers and dressing. Cover with plastic wrap and refrigerate for at least 2 hours before serving.

STEIRISCHER KRAUT SALAT

makes 6 to 8 servings

1 medium head of cabbage,
    cored and finely sliced
3 tsp. caraway seeds

Salt and pepper to taste
1 cup bottled Roquefort
    or other creamy dressing

In a bowl, combine the cabbage, caraway seeds, salt and pepper, and dressing. Cover with plastic wrap and refrigerate for at least 1 hour before serving.

SWISS-STYLE TOMATOES AND BRIE

makes 4 servings

1 wheel (4½ oz.—about
   3 inches in diameter)
   Brie cheese
1 tsp. pepper

1 can (7 oz.) baby
   pear tomatoes
1 tbsp. fresh savory, snipped

1. Lightly grease a 9-inch microwave-proof pie dish.
2. Place the cheese in the prepared dish, score the top in a diamond
   pattern, and sprinkle with pepper. Microwave on high heat for about
   2 minutes or until the cheese starts to melt.
3. Arrange the tomatoes around the cheese and cook on high heat
   for about 1 minute or until the tomatoes are thoroughly heated.
   Remove from the microwave, cut into wedges, garnish with savory
   and serve.

TOMATO SALAD

makes 4 servings

2 large beefsteak tomatoes,
  thinly sliced
¼ teaspoon sugar
2 scallions, trimmed
  and chopped

½ cup bottled French dressing
Cilantro, chopped

In a dish, arrange the tomato slices in overlapping layers. Sprinkle with the sugar and top with the scallions. Cover with plastic wrap and refrigerate for at least 1 hour. Drizzle on the dressing, garnish with cilantro and serve.

TROPICAL
SALAD

makes 4 to 6 servings

3 pink grapefruit, peeled
and separated into sections
1 large papaya, peeled,
seeded and thinly sliced
3 avocados, peeled,
seeded and thinly sliced

3 tbsp. olive oil
Salt and pepper to taste
Citrus zest

In a bowl, combine the grapefruit, papaya and avocado. Cover with
plastic wrap and refrigerate for at least one hour. Drizzle on the oil,
season to taste, garnish with citrus zest and serve.

WARMER ERDAPFEL SALAT (HOT POTATO SALAD)

makes 4 to 6 servings

1 cup chicken stock
3 pounds Idaho potatoes,
   boiled in skins
2 tbsp. white onions, minced

¼ cup oil to taste
1 teaspoon wine vinegar
Salt and pepper to taste

1. In a saucepan, bring stock to a boil.
2. Pare and slice the potatoes while still warm. Place in a bowl and pour the stock over them. Set aside for 30 minutes. Add the onions. Drizzle with the oil and vinegar, season to taste, and serve.

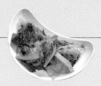

WILTED ROMAINE SALAD
WITH OYSTER SAUCE

makes 4 servings

2 tbsp. peanut oil
1 tbsp. premium oyster sauce

1 head of romaine lettuce,
separated

1. In a small bowl, blend together the oil and the oyster sauce.
2. In a two gallon-sized pot, bring lightly salted water to a boil.
   Dip the lettuce leaves in the boiling water for about 20 seconds
   and immediately dip them into a bath of cold water. Drain, and tear
   into bite-size pieces.
3. In a bowl, toss the lettuce with the oyster sauce and serve.

Cooking note: For variation, add seedless raisins.

PASTA WITH
ITALIANO SAUSAGE

makes 4 servings

1 pound Italian sausage,
  cut into ½-inch slices
3 cups bottled tomato sauce

1½ cups frozen mixed
  vegetables, thawed
  and drained
4 cups cooked pasta of choice

In a saucepan, sauté the sausage for about 10 to 15 minutes or until it loses its pinkish color. Drain the liquid, and add the tomato sauce and vegetables. Bring to a boil and reduce to a simmer. Cover and cook for about 10 minutes or until the vegetables are tender. Remove from the heat and serve with the pasta.

CANNELLINI BEANS MARINARA

makes 4 servings

1 bottle (30 oz.) tomato sauce
1 can (15 oz.) cannellini beans, drained
1 medium zucchini, trimmed, cut in half lengthwise and sliced

Cayenne pepper to taste
Salt and pepper to taste
1 package (8 oz.) pasta of choice, cooked and drained

In a large saucepan, combine the tomato sauce, beans, zucchini, and cayenne pepper. Bring to a boil and reduce to a simmer. Cover and cook, stirring occasionally, for about 20 minutes or until the zucchini is tender. Remove from the heat, season to taste, pour over the pasta, and serve.

MICROWAVE RICE
AND VEGGIES

makes 4 servings

1 cup instant rice
1 package (10 oz.) frozen
  mixed vegetables

3 tbsp. Tamari soy sauce

In a microwave-proof dish, combine the rice, 2 cups of water, and the vegetables. Cover and microwave on high heat for about 3 to 5 minutes or until tender and the liquid has been absorbed. Remove from the microwave, sprinkle with the soy sauce, fluff, and serve.

POLENTA-STUFFED PEPPERS

makes 4 servings

2 cups polenta, cooked
1½ cups whole kernel corn
6 oz. grated Monterey
  Jack cheese
Salt and pepper to taste

4 large red or green bell
  peppers, tops cut off and
  seeds and pith removed

1. Position the rack in the center of the oven and preheat to 350 degrees.
   Lightly grease an 8-inch square baking dish.
2. In a bowl, combine the polenta, corn, half of the cheese, and salt
   and pepper to taste.
3. Spoon into the peppers, sprinkle with the remaining cheese, and
   arrange in the prepared baking dish. Fill the dish halfway with water.
4. Cover and bake for about 10 minutes. Remove the cover and
   continue to bake for about 15 minutes or until tender and the
   cheese has melted. Remove from the oven and serve.

BEEF AND MACARONI

makes 4 to 6 servings

1 pound ground beef
½ cup light mayonnaise
1 can (30 oz.) tomato sauce

1 package (7 oz.) macaroni,
cooked and drained

1. In a skillet, sauté the beef for about 15 minutes or until lightly browned.
2. Blend in the mayonnaise and the tomato sauce and cover.
3. Simmer for about 10 minutes and add the macaroni. Cook for about 10 minutes or until thoroughly heated. Remove from the heat and serve.

Cooking note: For variation, use ground pork and beef mixed together and garnish with chopped mushrooms or olives.

CHINESE-STYLE PASTA SALAD WITH GINGER DRESSING

makes 4 to 6 servings

½ pound fresh shrimp, shelled and deveined
¼ cup ginger dressing
½ pound snow peas, cooked
2 tbsp. wine marinade

1 pound Shanghai noodles, cooked and drained, cut into 4-inch strands
1 tbsp. vegetable oil

1. In a bowl, combine the shrimp and the dressing. Cover with plastic wrap and refrigerate for about 1 hour.
2. In a wok, stir-fry the shrimp in the oil for about 7 minutes. Add the marinade, noodles, and peas. Stir-fry for about 5 minutes or until thoroughly heated. Remove from the heat and serve.

CREAMY TARRAGON PASTA

makes 4 servings

1¼ cups light cream
½ cup cream cheese,
   at room temperature

1 tbsp. dried tarragon
2 cups small shell pasta,
   cooked and drained

In the top of a double boiler over boiling water, combine the cream, cream cheese, and tarragon. Add the pasta and cook for about 5 minutes or until thoroughly melted. Remove from the heat and serve.

DESPERATE DAISY´S DINNER

makes 4 servings

2 cups bottled tomato sauce
1 garlic clove, minced
1 cup cooked broccoli florettes

2 cups wide egg noodles,
  cooked and drained

In a saucepan, cook the tomato sauce and the garlic for about 5 minutes.
Add the broccoli and noodles, and cook for about 5 to 10 minutes or
until thoroughly heated. Remove from the heat and serve.

EGGS AND MACARONI
FLORENTINE

makes 4 to 6 servings

2 packages (10 oz. each)
frozen chopped spinach,
thawed and drained
10 oz. macaroni,
cooked and drained

4 hard-boiled eggs, quartered
½ cup grated cheddar cheese
Salt and pepper to taste

1. Position the rack in the center of the oven and preheat to 350 degrees.
   Lightly grease a baking dish.
2. Layer the spinach, macaroni, hard-boiled eggs, and cheese in the
   prepared baking dish. Season each layer with salt and pepper to taste.
3. Bake for about 25 minutes or until the cheese has melted.
   Remove from the oven and serve.

FRUIT-FILLED
PASTA
makes 4 servings

2 cups pasta of choice,
  cooked and drained
1½ cups diced frozen
  fruit, thawed

1 cup Basic White Sauce
  (see below)
½ cup cherry tomatoes,
  quartered

In a bowl, combine the pasta, the fruit, the sauce, and the tomatoes.
Cover with plastic wrap and refrigerate for at least 1 hour before serving.

Cooking note: This dish can also be served hot.

BASIC WHITE SAUCE
makes 2½ cups

3 tbsp. butter
⅓ cup flour
2½ cup milk
salt and pepper to taste

In a saucepan, melt the butter and blend in the flour to make a roux.
Cook, stirring frequently, for about 1 minute. Blend in ½ cup of milk and
continue to cook, stirring frequently, for about 5 minutes or until smooth.
Blend in 2 cups of milk and continue to cook for about 5 minutes or until
thickened. Remove from the heat, season to taste, and serve.
Cooking note: The consistency of this sauce can be altered by the
amount of milk used.

FUSILLI WITH BROCCOLI AND GARLIC

makes 4 servings

½ cup sliced garlic
⅓ cup olive oil
4 cups broccoli florettes

1 pound fusilli, cooked and
  drained
Salt and pepper to taste

1. In a skillet, sauté the garlic in the oil for about 5 minutes or until
   tender. Add the broccoli and cook, stirring frequently, for about
   7 minutes or until just tender.
2. In a bowl, combine the pasta and broccoli. Season to taste and serve.

GREEK
MAKARONIA
makes 4 servings

1 stick (¼ pound) butter
   or margarine
¼ pound feta cheese, grated
1½ pounds spaghetti, cooked
   and drained

16 Greek Kalamata olives,
   pitted and chopped

1. In a saucepan, melt the butter and blend in the cheese. Cook for
   about 5 minutes or until thoroughly heated.
2. In a bowl, combine the pasta, cheese sauce, olives, and serve.

LAZY
LASAGNA TOSS

makes 4 servings

1 pound hot Italian sausages,
  casing removed and cut into
  bite-sized pieces
1 teaspoon olive oil
3 cups canned chunky
  spaghetti sauce

2½ cups cooked pasta
  shells or fusilli
Basic Parmesan Cheese Sauce
  (see below)

1. In a skillet, sauté the sausage in the oil for about 5 minutes or until it
   loses its pinkish color. Drain and add the tomato sauce. Cook for
   about 3 minutes or until the sauce starts to bubble.
2. In a bowl, combine the shells and the sausage mixture. Top with the
   cheese sauce and serve.

Cooking note: For variation, garnish with snipped oregano leaves.

BASIC PARMESAN CHEESE SAUCE

makes 4 servings

¾ cup Basic White Sauce (see p. 46)
¼ cup ricotta or cottage cheese
¼ cup grated fresh Parmesan cheese

In the top of a double boiler over boiling water, blend the sauce and the
ricotta cheese. Add the Parmesan cheese and cook for about 3 to 5
minutes or until the cheese has melted. Remove from the heat and serve.

MACARONI AND
BROCCOLI AU GRATIN

makes 4 to 6 servings

1 package (10 oz.) macaroni,
  cooked and drained
1½ cups blanched broccoli
  florettes, chopped

½ cup grated cheddar cheese
1 tbsp. pecans, chopped

1. Position the rack in the center of the oven and preheat to 350 degrees.
   Lightly grease a baking dish.
2. In a bowl, combine the macaroni and broccoli.
3. Arrange the mixture in the prepared baking dish and top with the
   cheese. Bake for about 20 minutes or until thoroughly heated and
   the cheese has melted. Remove from the oven, garnish with chopped
   pecans, and serve.

MACARONI
CHICKEN DINNER

makes 4 servings

2 cups elbow macaroni,
  cooked and drained
1 cup chicken,
  cooked and diced

1 can (10½ oz.) condensed
  cream of chicken soup
2 tbsp. white onions, diced

In a saucepan, combine the macaroni, chicken, soup, and onions.
Cook for about 10 minutes or until thoroughly heated. Remove from the
heat and serve.

MACARONI CHILI CASSEROLE

makes 4 to 6 servings

1 package (7½ oz.)
macaroni and cheese
1 can (10¾ oz.)cream of
mushroom soup, prepared
1 can (16 oz.) chili beans,
drained

1 can (3½ oz.) French's™
fried onions
1 tbsp. butter or margarine
½ cup milk

1. Position the rack in the center of the oven and preheat to 350 degrees.
   Lightly grease a 10 x 6-inch baking pan.
2. Arrange the pasta in the prepared baking pan. Pour in the soup, add
   the beans, and top with the onions. Bake for about 30 minutes or
   until thoroughly heated. Remove from the oven and serve.

MACARONI
CHILI DINNER

makes 6 servings

2 cups elbow macaroni,
   cooked and drained
1 can (15 oz.) chili with beans

1 can (10½ oz.) condensed
   tomato soup

In a saucepan, combine the macaroni, beans, and soup. Cook for about
10 minutes or until thoroughly heated. Remove from the heat and serve.

MACARONI
SAUTÉ

makes 4 to 6 servings

¼ cup broccoli florettes,
  blanched
¼ cup leftover bacon
  or meat drippings
1 package (8 oz.) macaroni,
  cooked and drained

1 tbsp. dried marjoram,
  crushed
Salt and pepper to taste

In a skillet, sauté the florettes in the oil for about 3 minutes or until
tender. Add the macaroni and sprinkle on the marjoram. Cook for about
5 minutes or until thoroughly heated. Remove from the heat, season to
taste, and serve.

Cooking note: For variation, use other vegetables instead of broccoli.

MACCHERONI
AL POMODORO
makes 4 servings

1 small yellow onion, diced
1 tbsp. butter or margarine
1 pound tomatoes, quartered

1 sprig of sweet basil
½ pound macaroni,
   cooked and drained

1. In a saucepan, sauté the onion in the butter for about 5 minutes
   or until tender. Transfer to a warming plate.
2. In the same saucepan, combine the tomatoes and the basil,
   and simmer for about 1 hour or until the tomatoes are reduced
   to a soft pulp. Drain and work the pulp through a sieve.
3. Pour the tomato pulp back into the saucepan, blend in the onions,
   and cook for 5 minutes or until thoroughly heated. Remove from the
   heat, pour over the pasta, and serve.

NOODLES
AND ASPARAGUS

makes 4 servings

⅓ cup butter or margarine
4 cups wide egg noodles,
  cooked and drained

2 cups fresh asparagus,
  cut into 1-inch pieces,
  cooked and drained

In a saucepan, combine the butter, noodles, and asparagus. Cook for about 10 minutes or until thoroughly heated. Remove from the heat and serve.

PASTA WITH SHRIMP AND TOMATO

makes 4 servings

1¼ pounds plum
   tomatoes, diced
16 large shrimp,
   cleaned and cooked

¼ cup fresh basil, snipped
2 garlic cloves, minced
1 package (10 oz.) spaghetti,
   cooked and drained

In a bowl, combine the tomatoes, shrimp, basil, and garlic. Pour over the pasta and serve.

PASTA WITH
VEGETABLE RIBBONS

makes 4 servings

1 package (8 oz.) tagliatelle
1 large carrot, trimmed, pared
  and cut into thin ribbons
1 medium zucchini, trimmed
  and cut into thin ribbons

1 tbsp. butter or margarine,
  room temperature
Salt and pepper to taste

1. In a saucepan, bring 1 quart of lightly salted water to a boil. Add the
   pasta and cook, stirring occasionally, for about 10 minutes or until
   the pasta is al dente. Add the carrots and zucchini, and cook for
   1 minute. Drain.
2. In a bowl, combine the pasta, vegetables, and butter. Season to taste
   and serve.

PASTA SMOTHERED
WITH ONIONS AND HAM

makes 4 servings

2 large onions,
  cut into thin rings
1 tbsp. butter or margarine
1 ham steak (about 1 to
  1½ pounds), cut into
  bite-size pieces

Oregano to taste
2 cups pasta of choice,
  cooked
¼ cup freshly grated
  Parmesan cheese

1. In a skillet, sauté the onions in the butter for about 5 minutes or until
   tender. Transfer to a warming plate.
2. In the same skillet, sauté the ham for about 15 minutes or until it
   loses its pinkish color. Stir in the onion and the oregano to taste.
3. Cook for about 10 minutes or until thoroughly heated. Remove from
   the heat, pour over the pasta, top with cheese, and serve.

PASTA WITH GARLIC
AND SHERRY

makes 4 servings

1 garlic clove, minced
⅓ cup olive oil
1 package (10 oz.) spaghetti,
cooked and drained

⅓ cup dry sherry
¼ cup grated cheese of choice
Salt and pepper to taste

1. In a saucepan, sauté the garlic in the oil for about 5 minutes or until tender.
2. Stir in the pasta and the sherry, and season to taste.
3. Cook for about 10 minutes or until thoroughly heated. Remove from the heat, top with cheese and serve.

PASTA WITH
SWEET POTATOES

makes 2 servings

1 package (10 oz.) frozen
  mixed vegetables,
  cooked and drained
½ cup cooked sweet potato,
  diced

¼ cup bottled fat-free
  dressing of choice
2 cups cooked shell pasta
Salt and pepper to taste

In a saucepan, combine the vegetables, sweet potato, dressing,
and pasta. Cook over low heat for about 10 to 15 minutes or until
thoroughly heated. Remove from the heat, season to taste, and serve.

PASTA WITH TAHINI SAUCE

makes 4 servings

1 package (8 to 10 oz.)
  pasta of choice,
  cooked and drained
1 cup green peas,
  cooked and drained

6 tbsp. bottled tahini sauce
1 tbsp. peanuts or toasted
  sesame seeds

In a bowl, combine the pasta, peas, and tahini. Garnish with peanuts or sesame seeds and serve.

Cooking note: For variation, add cooked shrimp.

RAMEN NOODLES
WITH CHINESE CABBAGE

makes 4 servings

2 packages (2½ oz. each)
  chicken ramen noodles
½ cup rice vinegar
½ cup sliced almonds, toasted

½ head of cabbage,
  thinly sliced
1 bunch scallions,
  trimmed and chopped

1. Cook the noodles according to the package directions (but reserve seasoning package) and drain.
2. In a small bowl, blend the contents of the seasoning package and the vinegar.
3. In another bowl, combine the almonds, cabbage, scallions, and noodles. Pour the vinegar mixture over the top and serve.

SHELLS WITH
SPINACH AND BEANS
makes 4 servings

1 package (10 oz.) frozen
chopped spinach, thawed,
cooked and drained
1 can (16 oz.) cannellini beans,
rinsed and drained

1 jar (16 oz.) tomato sauce
1¼ cups pasta shells,
cooked and drained

In a saucepan, combine the spinach, beans, and tomato sauce. Cook for
about 5 minutes or until thoroughly heated. Remove from the heat,
pour over the pasta, and serve.

SOBA NOODLES
WITH GARLIC

makes 2 servings

½ package soba noodles,
  cooked and drained
1 package (1½ oz.) soup mix
2 tbsp. scallions, minced

1 large clove garlic,
  peeled and minced
1 tbsp. sesame seeds

In a small bowl, combine the pasta, soup mix, scallions, and garlic.
Garnish with sesame seeds and serve.

SPAGHETTI PIE

makes 4 to 6 servings

1 package refrigerated
  pizza crust, uncooked
2 to 2½ cups leftover
  spaghetti with sauce

2 tbsp. sliced ripe olives
3 tbsp. grated cheese of choice

1. Position the rack in the center of the oven and preheat to 400 degrees.
   Lightly grease a 9 x 5-inch loaf pan.
2. Shape the crust to fit the prepared loaf pan. Fill the crust with the
   spaghetti, and top with the olives and cheese.
3. Bake for about 20 to 30 minutes or until the cheese has melted and
   the crust is light golden-brown. Remove from the oven, invert the
   pan onto a serving platter, slice, and serve.

SPANISH-STYLE PASTA WITH ONION SAUCE

makes 4 to 6 servings

1½ pounds yellow onions, sliced
1 cup butter or margarine
1 tbsp. sugar

¼ cup Madeira wine
1 package (16 oz.) pasta of choice, cooked and drained
¼ cup grated Romano cheese

1. In a saucepan, sauté the onions in the butter for about 5 minutes or until tender.
2. Add the sugar and cook over low heat, stirring occasionally, for about 1 hour.
3. Add the wine and cook for about 3 minutes or until heated.
4. Remove from the heat, pour over the pasta, sprinkle with the cheese, and serve.

THAI
FETTUCINI

makes 4 servings

1 can (14 oz.) Thai coconut milk
2 tbsp. curry powder
4 cups broccoli florettes,
  cooked and drained
1 large red bell pepper,

stemmed, seeded and diced
1 package (8 oz.) fettucini,
  cooked al dente and drained

In a bowl, combine the coconut milk and the curry powder.
Add the broccoli and the peppers. Pour over the pasta and serve.

ASIAN-STYLE
ALMOND-POPPY NOODLES

makes 4 servings

¼ cup slivered almonds
3 tbsp. butter or margarine
1 package (8 oz.) medium egg
  noodles, cooked and drained

1 tbsp. poppy seeds

In a skillet, sauté the almonds in the butter for about 5 to 7 minutes or until browned. Add the pasta and poppy seeds. Continue to cook for about 5 minutes or until thoroughly heated. Remove from the heat and serve.

HAM AND VEGGIE STIR-FRY

makes 4 servings

1 cup ham, cooked
  and chopped
2 tbsp. sesame oil
1 cup cooked shrimp
1 package (10 oz.) frozen
  mixed vegetables, thawed
  and drained

2½ cups cooked pasta
  of choice
Salt and pepper to taste

1. In a wok, stir-fry the ham in the oil for about 5 minutes or until well-coated with the oil.
2. Add the shrimp, stir-fry for about 1 minute and add the vegetables. Cook, stirring occasionally, for about 2 to 5 minutes or until the vegetables are just tender.
3. Add the pasta and season to taste. Cook for about 10 minutes or until thoroughly heated. Remove from the heat and serve.

Cooking note: For variation, serve with Oriental-style sauce on the side.

CHICKEN NUGGETS WITH HONEY AND MUSTARD SAUCE

makes 4 servings

2 boneless chicken breasts, cut into bite-size pieces
1½ cups bottled honey mustard sauce

½ cup crushed pretzels

1. Position the rack in the center of the oven and preheat to 375 degrees. Lightly grease a baking or cookie sheet.
2. Dip the chicken in the sauce, roll in the crushed pretzels, and arrange on the prepared baking sheet. Bake for about 15 to 20 minutes or until tender. Remove from the oven and serve with the remaining sauce on the side.

CHICKEN-STUFFED POTATO

makes 4 servings

1 large russet potato
1 package (4 oz.) frozen
  Chicken à la King

Salt to taste
Small bunch of chives,
  chopped

1. Scrub the potato and stab several times with a fork. Microwave on high for about 3 minutes.
2. Open the cooking pouch of the chicken, snip off a small corner of the package, and place in the microwave next to the potato. Microwave on high for about 3 to 4 minutes.
3. Cut the potato in half lengthwise—do not cut all the way through. Press the ends to open the potato. Sprinkle with salt and spoon the chicken into the potato. Sprinkle with chopped chives and serve immediately.

CHICKEN WITH
WINE AND MANGO

makes 8 servings

8 boneless chicken breasts,
  halved
½ cup dry white wine

¾ cup ripe mango,
  chopped

1. Position the rack in the center of the oven and preheat to 350 degrees.
   Lightly grease a shallow baking dish.
2. Arrange the chicken in the prepared baking dish and dot with the
   butter. Cover and bake, basting occasionally, for about 30 minutes.
   Remove the cover, add the wine, and continue to bake for about 15
   to 20 minutes, or until tender. Sprinkle with the mango and cook for
   about 3 minutes or until thoroughly heated. Remove from the oven
   and serve.

CRISPY CHICKEN

makes 6 servings

3 whole boneless, skinless, chicken breasts, halved
¾ cup Miracle Whip™ salad dressing

1 cup crushed corn flakes
½ cup grated Parmesan cheese
Salt and pepper to taste

1. Position the rack in the center of the oven and preheat to 350 degrees. Lightly grease a 13 x 9-inch baking pan.
2. Brush the chicken with salad dressing, dredge in the corn flakes, and roll in the cheese. Season to taste.
3. Arrange the chicken in the prepared baking pan and bake for about 60 minutes or until tender and lightly browned. Remove from the oven and serve.

HONEY´S
CHICKEN

makes 4 servings

2 tbsp. warm honey
½ teaspoon dried rosemary,
  crushed

Salt and pepper to taste
4 boneless chicken breasts,
  halved

1. Position the broiler rack about 6 inches from the heat.
   Lightly grease the broiler pan.
2. In a small bowl, blend together the honey and rosemary.
   Season to taste.
3. Brush both sides of the chicken with the honey-herb mixture and
   arrange on the prepared broiler pan. Broil for about 15 minutes.
   Turn over and broil for about 10 minutes or until tender.
   Remove from the oven and serve.

ORANGE-GLAZED
CHICKEN

makes 4 servings

¾ cup Italian dressing
½ cup orange marmalade
2 tsp. ground ginger

1 medium chicken (about
3 to 3½ pounds) cut into
serving-sized pieces

1. Position the rack in the center of the oven and preheat to 375 degrees. Lightly grease a 13 x 9-inch baking dish.
2. In a bowl, blend together the dressing, marmalade, and ginger.
3. Arrange the chicken, skin side up, in the prepared baking dish. Brush with the glaze. Bake, brushing occasionally, for about 1 hour or until tender. Remove from the oven and serve.

SWEET-AND-SOUR CHICKEN

makes 4 servings

1 can (8½ oz.) crushed
  pineapple in syrup
¼ cup prepared mustard
½ cup chopped chutney

1 medium (about 3 to 3½
  pounds) chicken, cut into
  serving-sized pieces
1 tbsp. butter or margarine
Salt and pepper to taste

1. Position the rack in the center of the oven and preheat to 350 degrees.
   Lightly grease a 13 x 9-inch baking pan.
2. In a bowl, blend together the pineapple (with syrup), mustard,
   and chutney.
3. Place the chicken in the prepared baking pan, season to taste, and
   pour the pineapple mixture over the top. Bake, basting occasionally,
   for about 1 hour or until tender. Remove from the oven and serve.

BROILED
SHRIMP SCAMPI

makes 3 servings

½ cup creamy garlic dressing
1 tbsp. lemon juice

1 pound fresh shrimp, cleaned,
shelled, and deveined

1. Position the broiler rack about 4 inches from the heat.
2. In a bowl, blend together the dressing and lemon juice.
3. Arrange the shrimp on the broiler pan and drizzle the dressing over the top. Broil, turning only once and basting, for about 7 to 10 minutes or until lightly browned.

CHILI
SHRIMP

makes 2 servings

3 tbsp. vegetable oil
½ pound fresh shrimp,
  cleaned, shelled,
  and deveined

1 large onion, sliced
3 tbsp. bottled chili sauce

In a wok, heat the oil and add the shrimp and onions. Stir-fry for about
3 minutes, and blend in the chili sauce. Continue to stir-fry for about 4
minutes or until the onions are lightly browned. Remove from the heat
and serve.

CHINESE-STYLE
SHRIMP FRIED RICE

makes 4 servings

3 large eggs, slightly beaten
1 to 2 tbsp. vegetable oil
1 can (4 oz.) chopped tiny
  deveined shrimp, drained
3 tbsp. rice wine

1 cup cooked rice, cold
Salt and pepper to taste
⅓ cup barbecued pork,
  cooked and chopped
½ cup soy sauce

1. In a skillet, fry the eggs in the oil, tilting the pan to spread the eggs
   as thin as possible. Remove from the heat and cut into narrow strips.
2. In the same skillet, sauté the shrimp for about 3 to 4 minutes or until
   thoroughly heated. Add the wine and the rice, and season to taste.
   Cook, stirring frequently, for about 2 to 3 minutes or until the rice is
   completely coated.
3. Add the pork and continue to cook, stirring frequently, for about 2 to
   3 minutes or until thoroughly heated. Remove from the heat and
   serve with the soy sauce on the side.

SIMPLE SWEET-AND-SOUR SHRIMP

makes 4 servings

3 cups rotelli pasta
1 package (10 oz.) frozen
cooked shrimp

1 package (10 oz.) frozen
Japanese-style vegetables
1 jar (9 oz.) sweet-and-sour
sauce

1. In a 3-quart microwave-proof casserole, blend together 1 cup of
water and the pasta. Cover and microwave on medium, stirring
occasionally, for about 10 minutes.
2. Add the shrimp and vegetables, cover, and continue to cook, stirring
occasionally, for about 5 to 8 minutes or until the pasta is al dente.
3. Stir in the sweet-and-sour sauce, and cook for about 2 minutes
or until thoroughly heated. Remove from the oven and serve.

FISH-POTATO
HASH

makes 2 to 4 servings

2 cups potatoes,
  cooked and diced
2 cups cooked fish, flaked

¼ teaspoon onion, minced
Salt and pepper to taste
1 tbsp. vegetable oil

1. In a bowl, combine the potatoes, fish, and onion, and season
   to taste.
2. In a skillet, heat the oil and add the fish and potato mixture.
   Cook over low heat until the bottom is browned. Remove from
   the heat and serve.

GRILLED WHITEFISH WITH TARRAGON SAUCE

makes 6 servings

½ cup bottled clam juice
3 tbsp. fresh lemon juice
3 tbsp. fresh tarragon, snipped
¾ cup olive oil

6 whitefish fillets with skin
(about 8 oz.)
Salt and pepper to taste

1. Position the grill about 6 inches from the heat.
2. In a saucepan, bring the clam juice to a boil for about 5 minutes, or until reduced to about 2 tablespoons.
3. In the container of a blender or food processor, combine the clam juice, lemon juice, tarragon, and oil. Process on high speed until smooth.
4. Place the fish on the grill, brush with a little oil, and season to taste. Grill without turning, for about 5 minutes, or until the fish becomes flakey. Remove fillets from the grill, drizzle with the sauce, and serve.

MUSTARD-GLAZED SALMON

makes 2 servings

¾ pound fresh salmon fillets	1 tbsp. Dijon mustard
1 tbsp. vegetable oil	Salt and pepper to taste
¼ cup balsamic vinegar	

1. In a skillet, sauté the salmon in oil on high heat for about 6 minutes or until both sides are lightly browned. Transfer to a warming plate.
2. In the same skillet, boil the vinegar on high heat for about 5 minutes or until most of the liquid has evaporated. Add the mustard and salmon, and season to taste. Cook for about 2 minutes or until thoroughly heated. Remove from the heat and serve.

SALMON CAKES

makes 6 servings

6 potatoes, cooked
  and chopped
2 cups canned salmon,
  skinned, boned and flaked
1 large egg

Pepper to taste
Celery salt to taste
¼ cup vegetable oil
Tartar Sauce (see below)

1. In a bowl, combine the potatoes, salmon, and eggs, and season to taste. Shape into 6 patties.
2. In a skillet, heat the oil and sauté the patties for about 10 minutes or until both sides are light golden-brown. Remove from the heat and serve with the Tartar Sauce on the side.

TARTAR SAUCE

makes ½ cup

½ cup mayonnaise
1½ tsp. lemon juice
½ teaspoon dried basil
Hot sauce (bottled) to taste

In a bowl, using a wire whisk or an electric mixer, blend the mayonnaise, lemon juice, basil, and hot sauce until smooth. Cover with plastic wrap and refrigerate for at least 1 hour before using.

SEARED
SALMON

makes 4 servings

4 salmon fillets
  (about 8 oz. each)
3 tbsp. vegetable oil

2 tbsp. vegetable relish
  of choice
Salt and pepper to taste

In a skillet, sauté the salmon in the oil for about 5 minutes or until sides
are browned. Remove from the heat, top with relish, season to taste
and serve.

BEAN-STUFFED SQUASH

makes 4 servings

2 medium large acorn squash,
  stemmed, seeded and halved
1 package (about 9 oz.)
  sliced green beans in butter
  sauce, prepared

3 tbsp. honey
¼ cup walnuts or pine nuts,
  chopped

1. Position the rack in the center of the oven and preheat to 350 degrees.
   Lightly grease a shallow baking dish.
2. Arrange the squash in the prepared baking dish cut-side down.
   Bake for 30 to 40 minutes or until tender.
3. In a bowl, combine the beans, honey, and walnuts.
4. Turn the squash cut-side up and stuff with the bean mixture.
   Bake for about 5 minutes or until thoroughly heated. Remove from
   the oven and serve.

HARVEST
SQUASH
makes 4 to 6 servings

1 acorn squash (about 1 ¼
  pounds), halved and seeded
1 tbsp. melted butter
  or margarine
1 package (10 oz.) frozen
  broccoli, cooked and drained

1 package (10 oz.) frozen
  carrots, cooked and drained
Salt and pepper to taste
½ cup shredded
  American cheese

1. Position the rack in the center of the oven and preheat to 400 degrees.
   Have a 12 x 9-inch baking dish available.
2. Arrange the squash halves in the baking dish cut-side down and bake
   for about 30 minutes or until tender.
3. Turn the squash cut-side up, drizzle with the butter and fill with the
   vegetables. Season to taste and sprinkle with the cheese. Continue to
   bake for about 3 to 5 minutes or until the cheese has melted.
   Remove from the oven, cut, and serve.

ROASTED SQUASH
WITH SPINACH AND CHEESE

makes 4 servings

2 acorn squash
  (about 1 pound each),
  halved and seeded
1 package (10 oz.) frozen
  chopped spinach, thawed
  and drained

1 cup shredded Gruyère cheese
¼ cup walnuts, chopped

1. Position the rack in the center of the oven and preheat to 400 degrees. Lightly grease a shallow baking tray.
2. Arrange the squash cut-side down on the prepared baking tray and bake for about 20 to 25 minutes or until tender.
3. In a bowl, combine the spinach, ¾ of the cheese, and the walnuts.
4. Turn the squash over and fill with the spinach mixture. Sprinkle the remaining cheese over the top and continue to bake for about 15 minutes or until the cheese has melted. Remove from the oven and serve.

EGGPLANT PARMIGIANA

makes 4 to 6 servings

2 small eggplants,
  trimmed, pared and
  cut into ½-inch slices
1 cup olive oil

1½ cups canned tomato sauce
½ pound Mozzarella cheese,
  thinly sliced

1. Position the rack in the center of the oven and preheat to 400 degrees.
   Lightly grease a 3-quart baking pan.
2. In a skillet, sauté the eggplants in the oil, turning occasionally, for
   about 10 minutes or until both sides are browned. Transfer to a rack
   covered with paper towels and drain.
3. Arrange half of the eggplants in the prepared baking pan, pour
   on half of the tomato sauce, and top with half of the cheese. Pour
   on the remaining sauce and top with the remaining cheese. Bake for
   about 15 minutes or until the cheese has melted. Remove from the
   oven and serve.

RATATOUILLE AU GRATIN

makes 4 servings

1 can (15 oz.) ratatouille   ¾ **cup grated cheddar cheese**
2 tbsp. red wine

1. Position the broiler rack about 4 inches from the heat.
   Have a shallow baking dish available.
2. In a saucepan, cook the ratatouille and the wine for about 2 minutes
   or until slightly heated.
3. Pour into the baking dish and top with the cheese. Broil for about
   10 minutes or until the cheese has melted. Remove from the broiler
   and serve.

SPINACH
LOAF

makes 2 to 4 servings

1 cup brown rice, cooked	1 tbsp. wheat germ
1 cup celery, chopped	2 cups spinach, cooked

1. Position the rack in the center of the oven and preheat to 400 degrees. Lightly grease a 6 x 4-inch baking pan.
2. In a bowl, combine the rice, celery, wheat germ, and spinach. Press into the prepared baking pan and bake for about 30 minutes or until thoroughly heated. Remove from the oven and serve.

SWEET POTATOES AND BROCCOLI

makes 2 to 3 servings

1 medium sweet potato,
  pared and diced
1 cup fresh broccoli, chopped

½ cup low-fat cottage cheese
1 tbsp. sesame seeds

1. In a saucepan, bring the potatoes and 1 cup of water to a boil and
   cook for about 15 minutes. Add the broccoli and reduce to a simmer.
   Continue to cook for about 5 to 6 minutes or until the potatoes
   are tender.
2. In a bowl, combine the potatoes, broccoli, cottage cheese, and
   sesame seeds, and serve.

TOMATOES STUFFED WITH SPINACH

makes 6 servings

2 cups spinach, cooked
1 tbsp. melted butter
or margarine
½ medium yellow onion,
minced

6 firm fresh tomatoes
½ cup grated cheese of choice

1. Position the rack in the center of the oven and preheat to 375 degrees. Lightly grease a 13 x 9-inch baking dish.
2. In a bowl, blend together the spinach, butter, and onion.
3. Cut the tops off the tomatoes, scoop out the centers, and fill with the spinach mixture.
4. Arrange in the prepared baking pan and bake for about 20 minutes or until the tomato skins start to wrinkle. Top with the cheese and continue to bake for about 10 minutes or until the cheese has melted. Remove from the oven and serve.

ZUCCHINI
PIE

makes 6 servings

4 cups zucchini, finely diced
½ cup yellow onion, minced
2 large eggs, beaten

½ cup bread crumbs
Salt and pepper to taste

1. Position the rack in the center of the oven and preheat to 375 degrees. Lightly grease a 9-inch pie plate.
2. In a bowl, combine the zucchini, onions, eggs, and bread crumbs, and season to taste.
3. Press into the prepared pie plate and bake for about 25 minutes or until tender. Remove from the oven, cut into wedges, and serve.

ZUCCHINI PIZZA

makes 6 servings

3 cups zucchini, grated,
drained and patted dry
3 large eggs, beaten
½ cup whole wheat flour

¼ teaspoon salt
1½ cups bottled tomato sauce
1 cup grated mozzarella
cheese

1. Position the rack in the center of the oven and preheat to 450 degrees.
2. On a flat, lightly floured surface, combine the zucchini, eggs, flour,
   and salt. Knead the dough until smooth and spread out to fit a
   12-inch round pizza pan.
4. Bake for about 20 minutes or until just firm. Remove from the oven
   and reduce the temperature to 350 degrees.
5. Spread the tomato sauce on the crust and top with the cheese.
   Bake for about 10 minutes or until the cheese has melted.
   Remove from the oven and serve.

Cooking note: For variation, add your favorite toppings.